Dinosaur Publications

Life in Ponds

by Althea
illustrated by Barbara McGirr

Published by Dinosaur Publications Ltd, Over, Cambridge, Great Britain

© text Althea Braithwaite 1984
© illustrations Barbara McGirr 1984
Made in Great Britain

ISBN 0 85122 411 3 (paperback)
ISBN 0 85122 412 1 (hardback)
Printed by Warners of Bourne + London

Pondskaters are probably the first animals you will see when you look into the pond or lake. They move about quickly and seem to slide across the top of the water. They are searching for food – smaller insects which have fallen into the water. Pondskaters are so light that the invisible film at the surface of water easily supports them. This film is almost like a skin, and the velvety hairs on the underside of the Pondskater's body protect it from the wet.

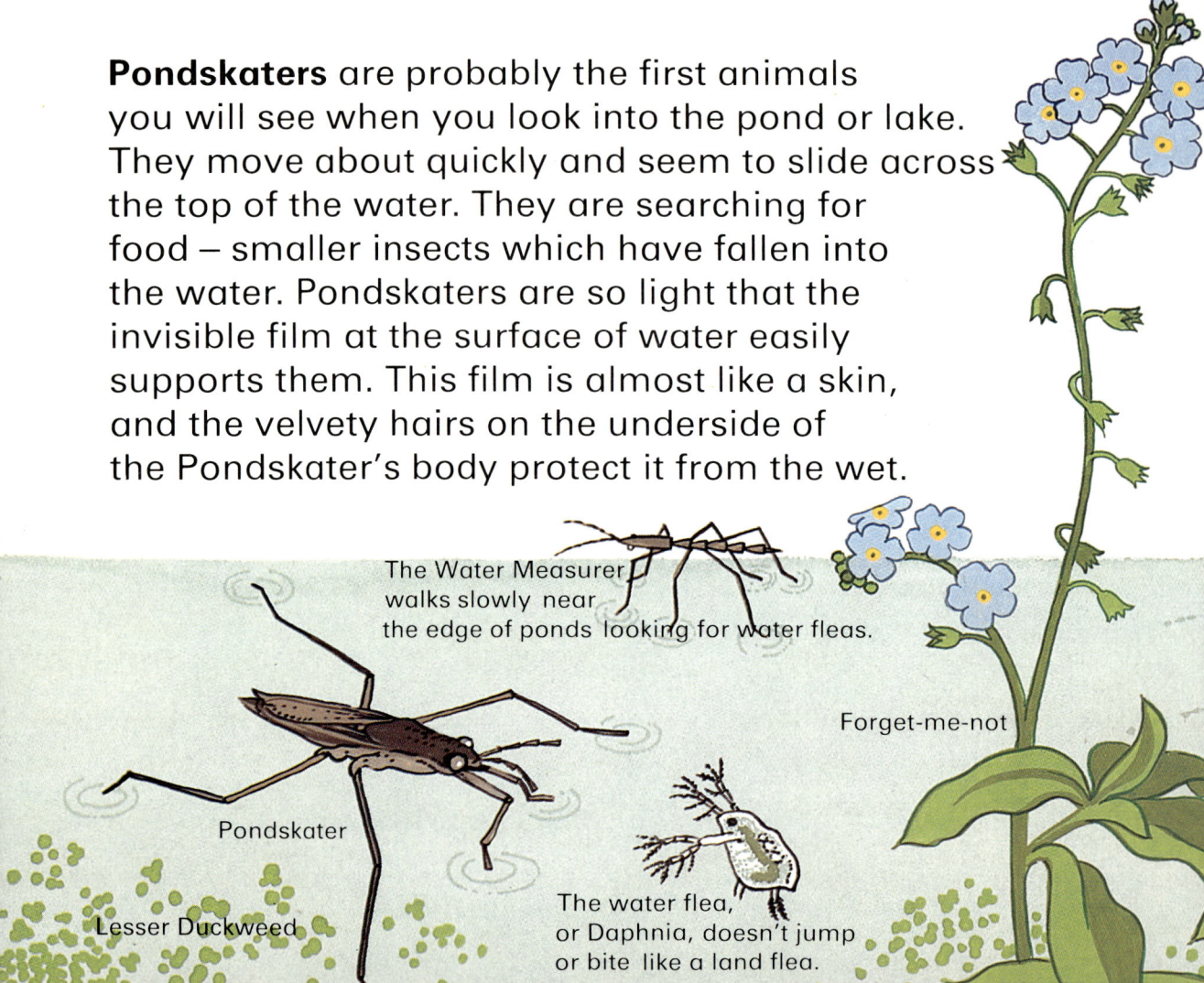

The Water Measurer walks slowly near the edge of ponds looking for water fleas.

Forget-me-not

Pondskater

Lesser Duckweed

The water flea, or Daphnia, doesn't jump or bite like a land flea.

Whirligig Beetles swim round and round
on the surface of the water. They use their
flat legs, which are fringed with hairs, like the
oars of a boat. Their eyes are in two parts –
one half for looking down into the water and the
other half for looking out for danger from above.
When they are frightened they dive very rapidly.
In cold weather, they bury themselves in the
mud at the bottom of the pond to keep warm.

Whirligig Beetles

Snails move around upside-down under the surface of the water searching for food. They breathe through a small hole under their shells, but they can also absorb oxygen from the water. Snails feed mainly on tiny green plants called algae. The **Great Pond Snail** eats dead animals too.

The Great Pond Snail lays its eggs in a mass of jelly which it sticks to the leaf of a water plant or to a stone. Many of the tiny newly hatched snails are eaten by other animals in the pond.

Freshwater Mussels and **Cockles** live in the mud right at the bottom of the pond. The Freshwater Mussel feeds by filtering water through its body and catching the tiny pieces of food that float in the water.

Snail's eggs

Great Pond Snail

Wandering Snail

Great Ramshorn Snail

Freshwater Mussel

Cockle

Some animals only live in the water for
a part of their lives.
Frogs and **Toads** will travel a long way
back to the water where they were hatched
to breed and lay their own eggs.

Frogs leap along in big hops but toads, with their shorter back legs, have to walk.

A female frog lays 2,000 or more eggs.
The eggs of frogs and toads have
a thick layer of jelly around them.
The jelly protects the eggs from the water.

Frogspawn

Toadspawn

After nearly two weeks the egg
develops into a tadpole which
wriggles its way out of the jelly.

Soon the tadpole grows hard jaws and
rows of tiny teeth to help it chew.
Its eats plants at first but later
it also feeds on tiny animals.

Tadpoles always grow their
back legs first.

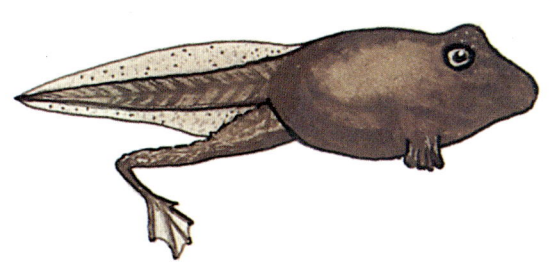

As its lungs grow inside, the tadpole slowly changes shape. After about ten weeks its front legs start to grow.

The tadpole can use its legs to walk along the bottom of the pond. As it grows older its tail gets shorter and shorter.

When the tail has completely gone, the tiny frog will be ready to leave the water. It won't become an adult and be ready to breed until it is three years old. Frogs eat snails, slugs and worms. They can also catch flies by flicking out their long tongues. In the cold of winter, frogs and toads find sheltered places to hibernate.

Newts also spend most of their time on land but return to the water to breed. The male's skin becomes more colourful and he grows a fin along the middle of his back to attract a female.
He may have to follow her around for several days, gently butting her with his head
before she takes any notice of him.

After the eggs have been fertilized, the female newt lays one on the leaf of a pond plant. Then using her back legs like hands, she folds the leaf over to protect the egg. For a month or so
she lays about ten eggs a day.

After about three weeks, each egg
develops into a newt tadpole,
which wriggles its way out of the jelly.
The baby newt – about 8mm long –
starts to feed on tiny animals which
it hunts at the bottom of
the pond.

The front legs of the tadpole
grow first. When its back legs
have grown, it can crawl around
the bottom of the pond among
the plant stems hiding from enemies.

By the end of the summer,
most of the tiny young newts
will have crawled out of the pond
to shelter under nearby stones.
A few late tadpoles may stay
in the pond for the winter.

Although the **Water Spider** lives underneath
the water, it still needs to breathe air.
It weaves a fine web under the water,
and then collects bubbles of air
from the surface and traps them under the web.
These bubbles push up the centre of the web to make
a safe, dry, airy tent for the spider to live in.
It rushes out from its tent to catch and eat
passing insect larvae and other small animals.

In Spring, the male spider builds a tent
next door to the home of a female. He then
makes an air tunnel through to her tent.
After mating, she lays about 50 to 100 eggs.
She stays in her tent to guard the eggs and
look after the young spiders when they hatch.
When the spiders are about a month old they
will go off to build their own homes.

Great Diving Beetles are not very
welcome in small garden ponds because
they will attack and eat newts
and even small goldfish.
But they are difficult to keep away because
the female flies through the night to lay
her eggs in the pond of her choice.

Each egg is laid in the stalk of a water plant.
The very fierce larva, which is nicknamed
'Tiger of the Pond', hatches in the Spring.
It feeds by sucking the blood from tadpoles
and other water creatures. It grows quickly,
shedding its skin as it gets bigger.
It leaves the water to pupate in the muddy bank.
In a few weeks it will turn into an adult beetle.

The Great Diving Beetle has come to the surface to collect air which it stores underneath its wings.

Larva of Great Diving Beetle feeding on a tadpole.

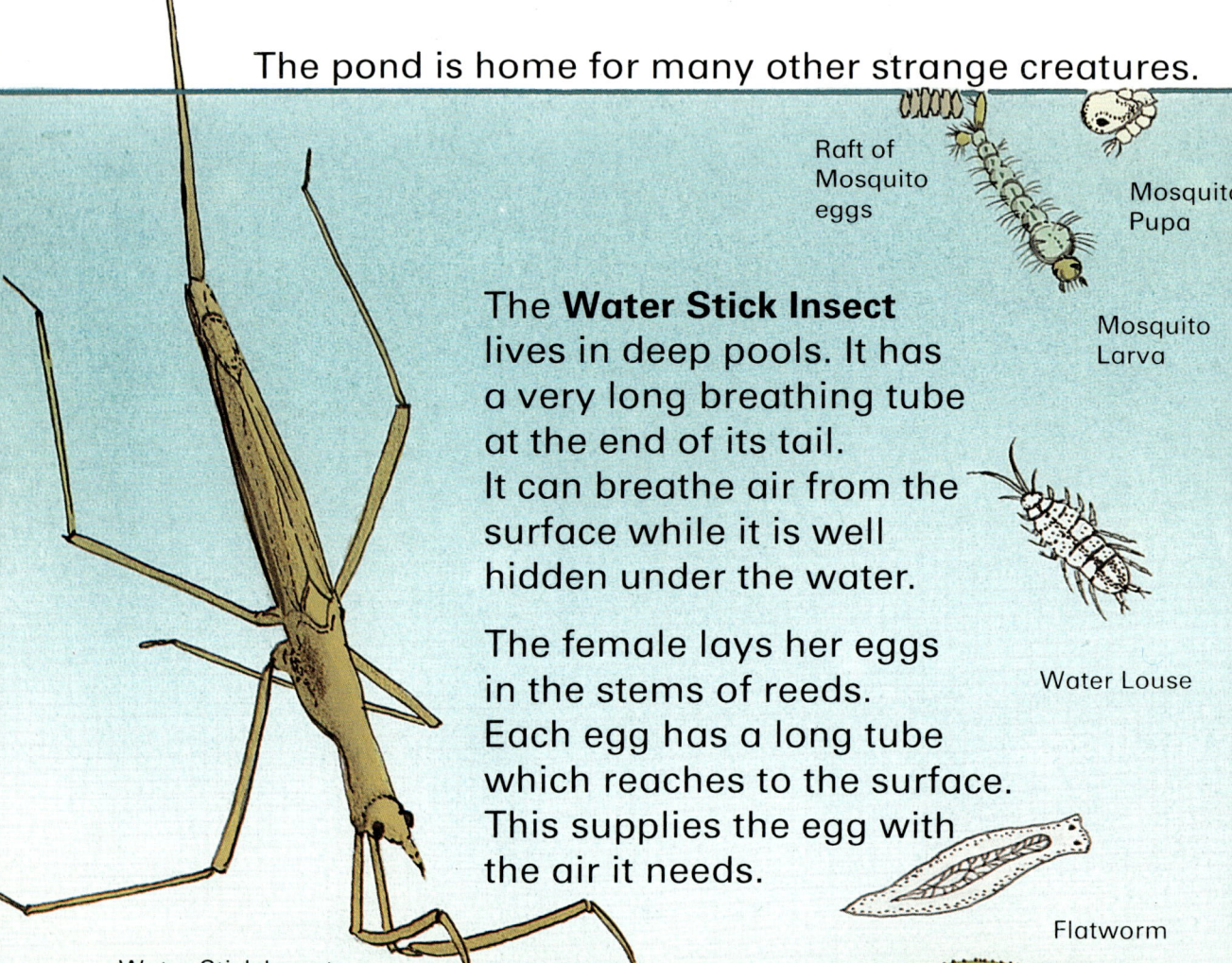

The pond is home for many other strange creatures.

Raft of Mosquito eggs

Mosquito Pupa

Mosquito Larva

The **Water Stick Insect**
lives in deep pools. It has
a very long breathing tube
at the end of its tail.
It can breathe air from the
surface while it is well
hidden under the water.

Water Louse

The female lays her eggs
in the stems of reeds.
Each egg has a long tube
which reaches to the surface.
This supplies the egg with
the air it needs.

Flatworm

Water Stick Insect

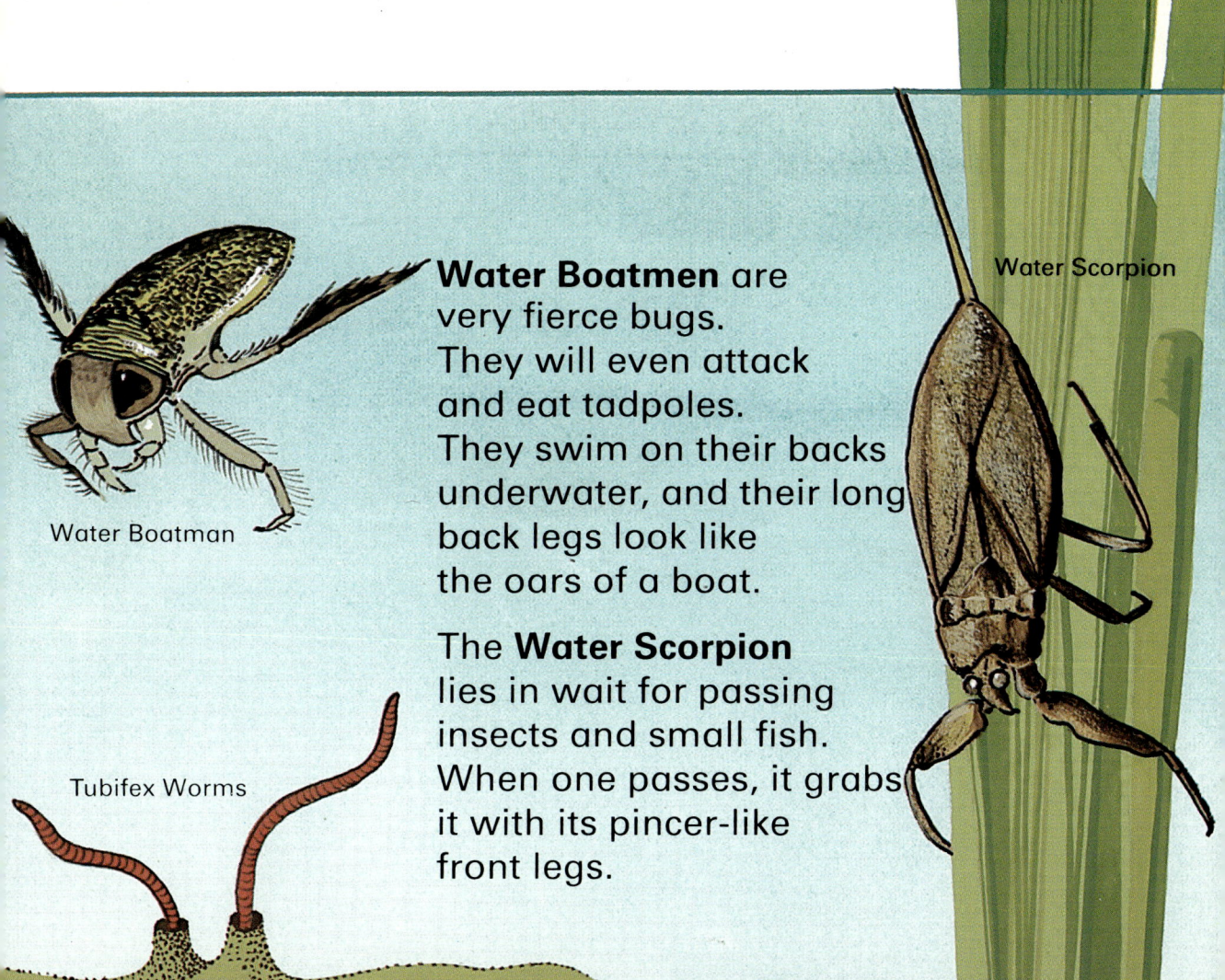

Water Boatmen are very fierce bugs. They will even attack and eat tadpoles. They swim on their backs underwater, and their long back legs look like the oars of a boat.

The **Water Scorpion** lies in wait for passing insects and small fish. When one passes, it grabs it with its pincer-like front legs.

Water Boatman

Tubifex Worms

Water Scorpion

These are some of the plants which grow in fresh water. Because the water carries the weight of the plant, many only have slender stems. Some have roots to anchor them to the bed of the pond and others float about in the water.

The **Water Soldier** has sharp sword-like leaves, it usually grows under the water, but it comes above to flower.

Hornwort has no roots at all. It flowers under the water.

These **Water Plantain** flower between July and September.

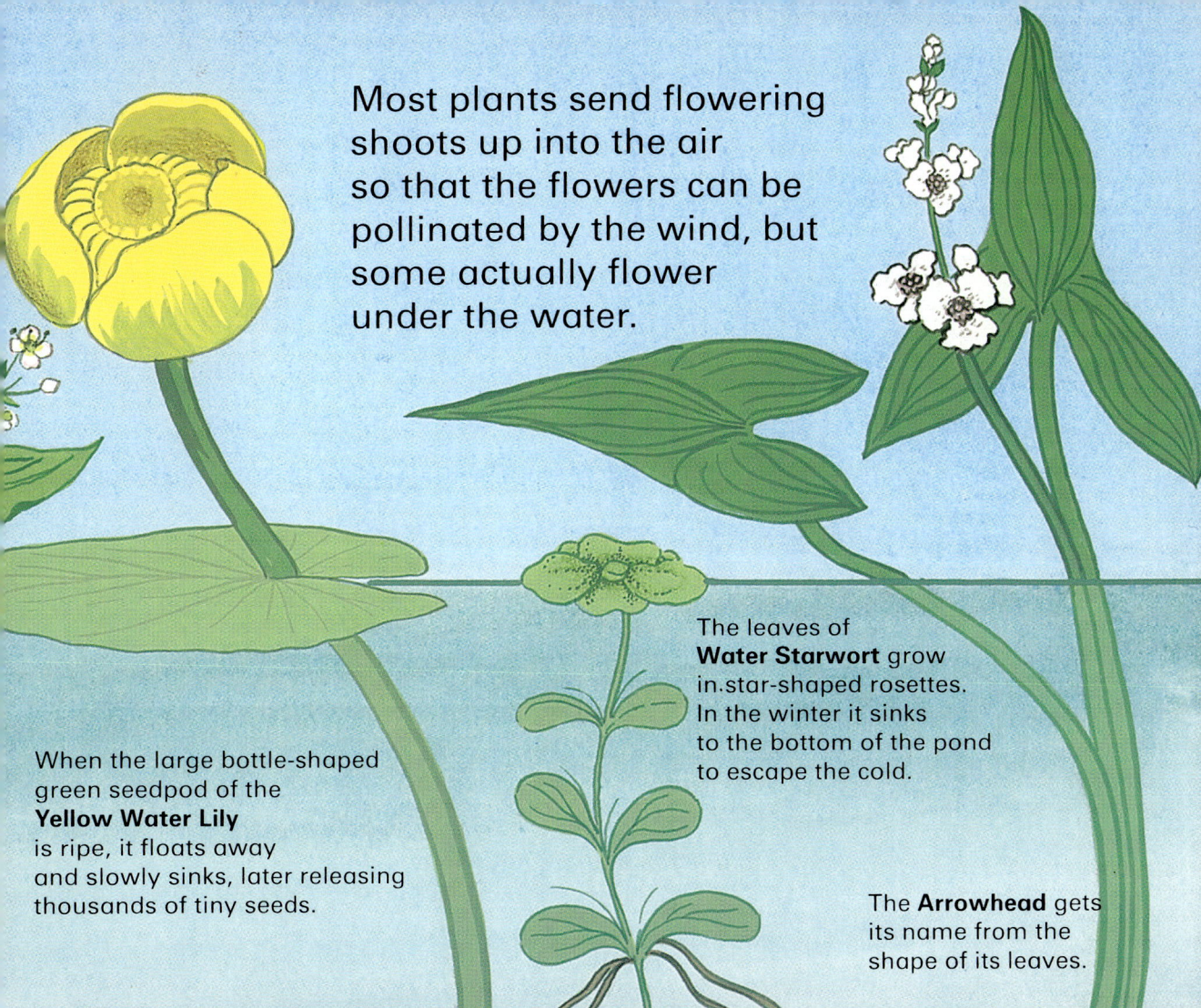

Most plants send flowering
shoots up into the air
so that the flowers can be
pollinated by the wind, but
some actually flower
under the water.

The leaves of
Water Starwort grow
in.star-shaped rosettes.
In the winter it sinks
to the bottom of the pond
to escape the cold.

When the large bottle-shaped
green seedpod of the
Yellow Water Lily
is ripe, it floats away
and slowly sinks, later releasing
thousands of tiny seeds.

The **Arrowhead** gets
its name from the
shape of its leaves.

The **Dragonfly** nymph will live in the pond for a year or more, feeding on small animals and even tadpoles. When it is ready to change into a dragonfly, the nymph climbs up a reed and out of the water. Then it sheds its last skin. It has to wait for several hours for its wings to expand and dry before it can fly away.

Damselfly

Dragonfly nymph shedding its skin.

The dragonfly nymph catches an unwary tadpole.

Dragonfly laying eggs

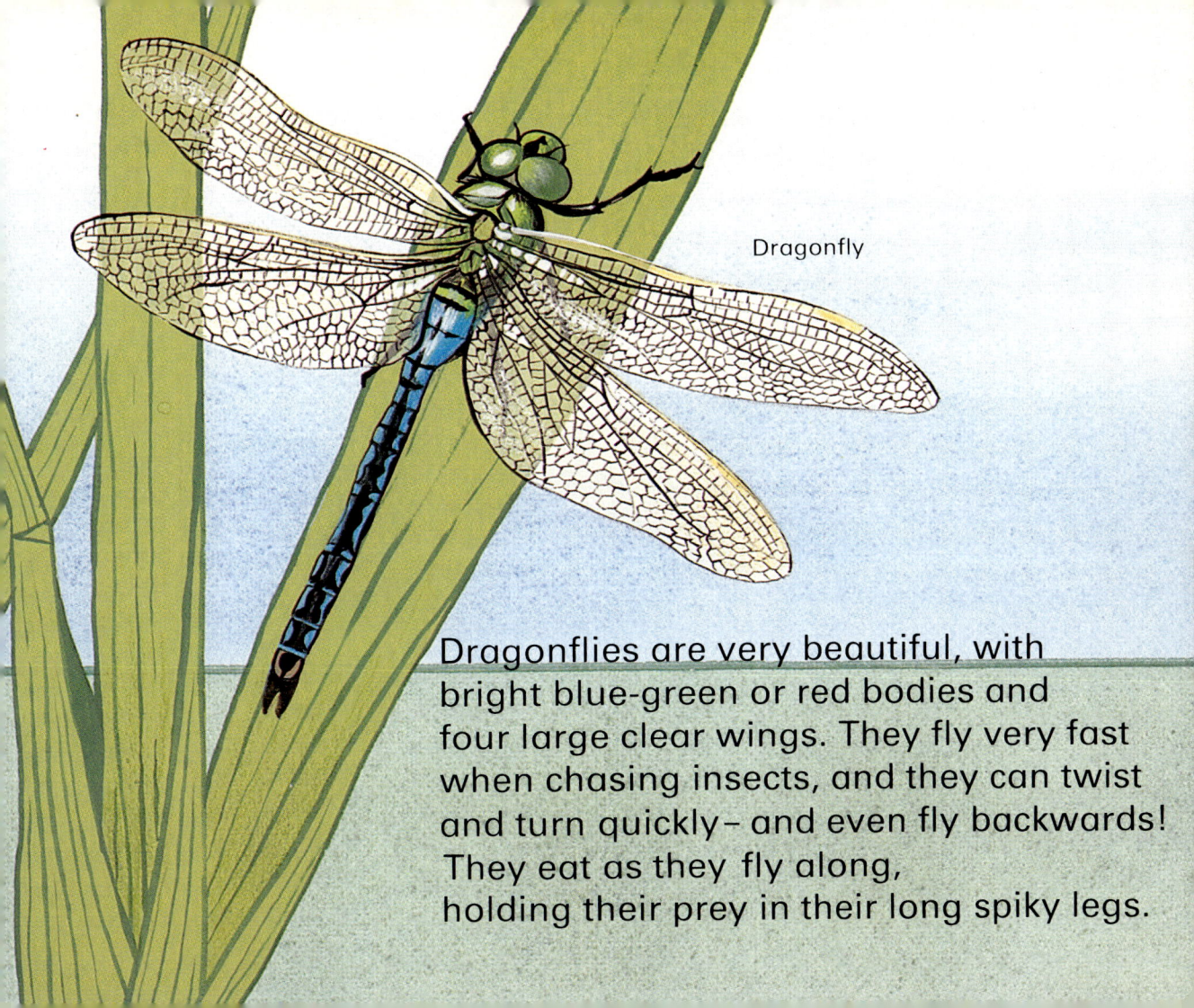

Dragonfly

Dragonflies are very beautiful, with
bright blue-green or red bodies and
four large clear wings. They fly very fast
when chasing insects, and they can twist
and turn quickly – and even fly backwards!
They eat as they fly along,
holding their prey in their long spiky legs.

Ducks are not the only birds which live on water.
Coots and **Moorhens** may also be seen swimming
near the rushes on a large pond or lake.
They build nests on the water.
Coots have only one family each season
but moorhens may have up to three families.
The older moorhen chicks help to look after
the babies.

Moorhen

Chick

Older chick

Coot and chicks

Moorhen

The Moorhen feeds on the surface and usually only dives when it is frightened.
Coots dive down to eat insects and plants and then bob up again in another place.
Both birds can swim well under the water.

Coot

Glossary

larva   stage of insect between egg and pupa

nymph   larva of Dragonfly or aphid – the young stage
of some insects can be called nymph or larva

pollinate   fertilize a plant with pollen
so that fruit will grow

pupate   change from larva into pupa or chrysalis